Cleaning Covid

Cleaning Covid

My MIS Adventures in

Dangerous Housekeeping

by Diane Delaney

Copyright © 2022 Diane Delaney.

All rights reserved.
No part of this book may be reproduced or used in any manner without written permission of the copyright owner except for the user of quotations in a book review.
The stories in this book reflect the author's recollection of events. Some names, locations, and identifying characteristics have been changed to protect the privacy of individuals. Dialogue has been recreated from memory.

Illustrations by the author.

isbn: 978-0-578-31462-4

CONTENTS

DEDICATION

This book is dedicated to every housekeeper with whom I had the honor and good fortune to work.

Covid is afraid of you because you carry in yourself the heart of a lion.

ACKNOWLEDGMENTS

Thank you Elite Authors for your editing and cover design services. And a shout out to my husband, R. Siiter, for all his support.

WRITER'S NOTE

I HAVE THREE APOLOGIES TO get off my chest.

The first is that I refer to Covid as being male. This is how I envision the character in this book. Gentleman, it's nothing personal.

The second apology is how I describe patients in the hospital who are suffering with Covid. I use the words "a Covid patient." In my daily parlance, I would say, "a patient with Covid."

The third is that parts of this book you may find funny. Covid isn't funny. Everyone knows that. However, the alarming and bottomless pit of my ineptitude shines through as I attempt to assist disciplined, first-class housekeepers.

—Diane Delaney

PREFACE

IT'S SPRING IN NEW JERSEY and the year is 2020. Television news crews, with cameras perched on their shoulders and plastic over their microphones, are interviewing a nurse in Saint's Hospital emergency room.

Interviewer: "How's it going today?"

Nurse: "It's crazy. There's no room to put all these people who are so sick."

Interviewer: "What's the plan?"

Nurse: "We just," she looks around at the chaos and continues, "we just keep going."

Interviewer: "Thank you for all you are doing."

The nurse, swaddled to the top of her head in white protective equipment, watches the TV crew bumping their way toward the exit and wonders, "Am I in hell?"

Unfortunately, the answer is yes. This lovely human was in hell – not the biblical hell we all know and don't love – but a new hospital hell, called Covid.

Shortly after that interview I worked in that hospital hell too. Yup, through no fault of my own, I was plopped right into the middle of the chaos. The stories in this book detail that experience.

PUSHED OUT OF THE NEST

For many years I worked in a doctor's office about a mile from Saints' Hospital in New Jersey. I was a simple dietitian. I had a simple life. I walked into work at 9:00 am, and at 5:00 pm on the dot I walked out of work with each hair on my head neatly in place.

Everything changed, however, when in March of 2020 a virus called Covid waltzed into the main lobby of Saints' Hospital, dropped his briefcase on the floor and looked around with a smile. "I'm Covid. I'm here," he said, pulling his gloves off one finger at a time, "and I'm never, ever, going to leave."

Due to this surprising and most unpleasant arrival of Covid, people who would ordinarily be scheduling appointments to come to the office to see me stopped making appointments. Instead, they were in their homes pushing heavy furniture against every door and window to bar Covid from breaking in.

I wished I could have been home doing the same. In fact, my husband and I enjoy playing catch with the occasional armoire. However, I did need a paycheck, so I continued to show up for work every day.

It didn't bother me that I was twiddling my thumbs; however, it did concern my office manager. One Friday in late March at 4:00 pm she stood in my office wringing her bony hands. She was a tiny woman nearing seventy who bred miniature dachshunds, and her face had a striking resemblance to that of her tiny canines.

"You don't have any patients coming in for appointments," she said, "and what's worse is that you don't have any patients scheduled for months." She was right and was pointing out something that I had noticed but was trying to ignore. I had not seen a patient in my office for a couple weeks.

"Marion, I think they'll be back soon," I said.

"When?" she asked and sat down at the round table in my office.

She didn't expect an answer. Covid held all the answers now and wasn't about to squeal. Until Covid was backed into a corner and handcuffed, no one was about to risk their life coming in to see me for calorie counting. Covid was everywhere and into all of it. He could be sitting here in my office, right now, biting on an eraser.

My boss, Marion Sanger, was a constant worrier. Last year I told her manager that he should pay Marion overtime for all the worrying about work that she does at home. He thought that was funny, but I meant it. Employees who worry are always underpaid.

I scrolled through my dietitian schedule on my laptop. "Look, Marion," I said trying to cheer her up, "I have a patient scheduled to see me the day before Thanksgiving. November will be here before you know it."

She had her elbows on the little round table and her face was resting in the palms of her hands.

"I'm sorry that I'm not six feet away from you," she said through clenched teeth, "and not socially distanced."

"It's okay," I said.

A few moments passed and Marion picked up her head. "I have bad news," she said picking at a cuticle. "I have to close this office." She stopped picking at her cuticle, put her chin back on her palms and stared at a plant.

Close the office? I stopped breathing. Covid does that to people, whether you are infected with the virus or not. Every person I know stops breathing at least five times a day. Someone stops breathing when they see soaring death rates pop up on their phone, while someone in the supermarket stops breathing when another shopper gets too close. Covid is small but mighty.

Closing the office was bad news. In a flash, my overweight mortgage sauntered into the office, winked at me, and sauntered out. I really needed this job. Last week in the silence of my office, I had calculated what unemployment might fork over, and it was not pretty.

"As of this morning," she said, slowly standing, "95% of the beds in Saints' Hospital are filled with patients who have Covid. Every minute there are lines and lines of cars at a dead stop outside the emergency room. Covid's in every car." Marion fell into her chair as though she were being pushed down. "Last night two people died in their cars waiting for help. They didn't even get into the emergency room."

Everyone knew that people were pouring into Saints' Hospital begging for oxygen.

Marion continued, "The hospital has tripled the housekeeping department budget and is pleading for employees to sign up with them." She was at her cuticles again. "You'll get the same pay as you do here," she added.

I think my boss was shipping me over to housekeeping. "You want me to go to housekeeping?"

She corrected herself, "It's actually called environmental services, also known as EVS."

"It doesn't matter what the department is called. I can't go, Marion," I said firmly. "First, I don't want to die." I thought that was a reasonable defense. "And second, I can't clean anything that's really dirty. It makes me feel bad." That was true. I hated gunk.

"Of all the people in this office, why send me to housekeeping? I can stay home on vacation pay." I also wanted to mention to her that I'm an aging, absent-minded woman who will be lips to lips with Covid as soon as I walk into the hospital lobby. "I can't do this, Marion," I said. "I'm sorry, but I'm not going to work in housekeeping in the hospital." That was that.

"Diane," she said, "If you do not do this, you may not have a job to come back to."

Crap.

"Here," she said and handed me this notice.

<u>NOTICE OF FURLOUGH TRANSFER</u>

DEPARTMENT: **ENVIRONMENTAL SERVICES**
EMPLOYEE: **DIANE DELANEY**
EMPLOYEE NUMBER: SH324776B

COMMENCE: Saturday, April 6, 2020
SHIFT: Third Shift 11:00 pm to 7:00am
Saturdays through Wednesdays

Employee ID must be worn. Face mask required.
Automobile ID sticker required on left rear window
Parking available in lot C.

Double crap.

ESTHER AND JERMAINE

THAT SATURDAY AT 10:45 PM I dragged myself into the main lobby of Saints' Hospital. Compared to the dark and quiet night, the hospital was ablaze with light and activity.

Last month a visiting dignitary was invited to tour the hospital after the lobby underwent a million-dollar face lift. After the tour she was interviewed by a local reporter and was quoted as saying, "The new Saints' Hospital lobby is impressive. The ceiling is high and curved like a cathedral." The hospital administration enjoyed that description and probably wished the interview stopped there. Unfortunately, she continued, "The problem with the hospital layout is that the beautiful lobby funnels down into four floors of mazes, dead ends, and stairwells that lead nowhere." An accurate but regrettable article.

I was looking up at the cathedral ceiling when a chipper volunteer called me to her table, squeezed sanitizer gel into my palms, took my temperature, and rushed me through the prerequisite Covid questions. Then a security guard offered to bring me downstairs to the basement where environmental services (EVS) is located.

"Do you have a map I can have of the hospital layout?" I asked.

"What do you mean, a map?"

"A map? A map is a piece of paper that says this is this and that's there," I told him helpfully.

"We stopped giving those out after 9/11 because we don't want terrorists to know where things are."

This was a silly argument for not providing maps. First, I doubt a terrorist would stop at a security station and ask for a map. Second, even if a terrorist did get hold of one, it would likely be indecipherable being the 10,000th copy of the original.

"Okay," I said and followed him to EVS downstairs.

The housekeeping department was a long, slim, dark corridor lined with gray cinder blocks. There were a few overhead lights, but the bulbs had burned out, especially at the far end of the corridor. Having a width of no more than ten feet makes social distancing a challenge, to say the least. And, as we all know, there is nothing Covid likes better than a bunch of people shoulder to shoulder.

This corridor was made even narrower due to several six-foot-long tables lining the walls. Each table was piled high with aluminum trays of Italian, Chinese, and Indian food, wobbly towers of half-filled pizza boxes, bags of donuts, plastic containers of salad, boxes of protein bars, chocolate bars, bars of soap, cookies, cakes, hand sanitizer, stacks of bottled water, and shoeboxes filled with small stones painted with sayings such as, "Stay Strong," "God Bless You," and "Thank You."

I saw that a line was forming along the wall to the right, so I walked over there and tapped on the shoulder of the woman at the end of the line.

"I'm a furloughed dietitian. Is this the line for environmental services?"

"Do you mean housekeeping?" she asked.

I nodded, and she motioned for me to stand behind her.

The line continued to grow behind me with employees in dark gray uniforms with "Environmental Services" embroidered in bright yellow above the left breast pocket. The woman in front of me turned around and complained to me about the line not moving.

I checked my watch. It was 11:15 pm, and we were still rooted in the same spot. Was I in the right place? I pulled the furlough notice out of my pocket and unfolded it. Unfortunately, it was not the furlough notice; it was the recipe for pistachio pudding pie I had printed earlier at home.

Everyone in the line was complaining about the delay when a woman, who must have been a supervisor, stepped out from the front of the line. Through two tight masks that were severely pressed against her nose and mouth she called out something that sounded a lot like, "Eat your nuts in soup!" She said it again, and the line started to move.

Reaching the front of the line, I stood facing the woman with the double masks. In her thirties, with black hair tied neatly in a bun, she wore the EVS uniform under a black cardigan sweater.

She stood behind a card table that had a metal tackle box on it. The box was open with the metal shelves and little compartments overflowing with keys. Leaning over to have a good look at me, she asked me a question that I couldn't understand.

"What?" I asked.

She asked the question again, but her masks were too thick and tight over her mouth.

"I can't understand you," I said.

She pulled her two masks down below her chin and said loudly, "How was your donning and doffing training?"

"What's that?"

"It's training you need," she said, rearranging two sets of keys in the tackle box. "You need training so you can don and doff before we send you up to the Covid units. It's why you're here."

"So that's why I'm here. I thought I'd be making beds and emptying garbage."

"Didn't anybody tell you what you're here for?" she asked.

"I'm a furlough."

"I know you are," she said, squinting her eyes and leaning across the table to read my ID badge.

I fished for a little sympathy saying, "This is my first time here. I'm lost."

"We're all lost, honey, you have to move on."

"But where to? I'm a furlough."

"You told me that already."

This woman was exhausted, but not the usual "I work too many hours" kind of exhaustion. This was Covid exhaustion—the crushing exhaustion we all wake up with whether we've slept twelve hours or two. I saw it in Marion's face yesterday in the office. I saw it last night in the employee who helped me find grape tomatoes in the produce section of my supermarket. I saw it this afternoon in the face of the young man filling tanks at the gas station. And here it was again in this young woman standing before me.

Esther

Covid has thrown a hard cloak, lined with lead, over all our shoulders.

Pointing behind her, she asked, "Do you see that man down there?"

"I think so."

"Go see him," she said, and slammed the door on our little chat.

The man at the end of the hallway was Jermaine Washington, a lanky man well over six feet tall in his forties who manages the 11:00 pm to 7:00 am housekeeping shift. After Covid moved into the hospital, his staff mushroomed and was still growing.

Leading his troops around Covid land mines every night is a thankless task, and as if this weren't enough misery for one man, each week he's saddled with a new crop of furloughs whose last sighting of a mop and pail was on the movie channel during Navy week.

"You're here," he said looking at me. "You must be Diane, our lost lamb. We've been waiting for you."

Balancing his laptop on his palm he said, "Now that all ten of you are here, let's go into the classroom."

He snapped his laptop closed, and we followed him into a large room with cinder block walls painted in pale yellow and four tracks of outdated fluorescent lighting. At least it was brighter than the corridor.

Tucked into a corner in the back of the room was a small kitchen, its counter buried under empty pizza boxes and a mini-fridge gurgling underneath.

We sat on folding chairs that had been set six feet apart.

"Let me introduce myself. I am Jermaine Washington, director of the 11:00 pm to 7:00 am shift here in environmental services."

He placed his laptop on a wooden desk in the front of the class and then leaned back against the desk, crossing his arms.

"As you all know," he started, "Covid challenges us every day to keep our patients safe." Looking up at the ceiling, he cleared his throat, continuing, "We have to stay safe also."

"Each night," he said lifting himself up from the desk, "each one of you will be paired with an experienced housekeeper, and that housekeeper will be relying on you to keep him or her safe."

"I heard a housekeeper died last night from Covid. Is that true?" the woman next to me said abruptly.

"Yes, that's true," Jermaine said looking down at his feet. "Yes," he repeated and sat down again on the desk.

"What happened?" she asked.

"He caught Covid last month… in March… when not much was known… We didn't know how far-reaching this would be." Jermaine was right. Covid netted a lot of the first responders.

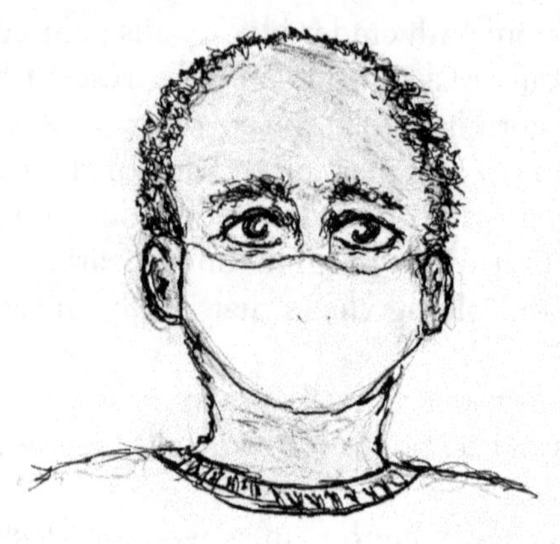

She persisted, "How did the guy die?"

Among my overflowing fountain of flaws is a tendency to get mixed up in any local argument.

"The poor guy died of Covid," I said looking at her. "He just said that."

"But was it… well, did he suffocate?" She stood up and faced Jermaine, who was visibly shaken.

"Maybe we shouldn't talk about this right now," I said, looking up at the woman.

"If not now, when? Think about it," the woman persisted loudly, twisting around to look at everyone. "We... every single one of us will be up there with Covid who'll be this far away from us." She was holding her palms six inches apart. "Don't you want to know how the housekeeper died? Do you want to die? I don't want to die," she repeated this a few times.

"We'll be okay," I said lamely. "We'll wear masks and uh—"

She interrupted, "So, masks are good now, huh? We're supposed to wear masks now? Why was it that last week we didn't have to wear masks? What about that, huh?"

In spite of her obnoxious tone, she had a good point.

In normal situations, we know who our enemy is and can usually figure out where they're hiding.

During World War II the Allied soldiers and the Axis soldiers were enemies. They saw each other, heard each other, and probably smelled each other. The Allied powers won the war for many reasons — not least among them was their consensus that the Axis powers did exist and that weapons, such as guns and bombs, were the means to destroy them.

Tackling the problem of Covid is complicated because we cannot see it. I've never seen a photo of Covid knifing someone in a train station. Have you? Furthermore, if we cannot see Covid, how will we agree on the means to destroy it? Get nine Americans in a room and ask them about Covid. Three of the nine are wearing a mask for protection, three more are chugging down antimalarial pills with a shot of bleach, while the last three believe Covid does not exist.

The woman turned to look at Jermaine and raged, "You send people up there and they die. Think about that! Do you ever think about how selfish that is?"

Let's all think about this for a minute. As far as I was concerned, she scored another point. Jermaine, who is safe down here in housekeeping, was about to send us up to the hospital to clean Covid while Covid's up there licking his lips and ready to pounce.

Jermaine might have been able to defend himself against her accusations if he paraphrased a well-known quote made by U.S. General Colin Powell. But it's likely this quote was not on the tip of Jermaine's tongue.

Powell said, "It takes more courage to send men into battle than to fight the battle yourself."

As gallant as that may sound, it has the tone of sweet surrender to us chickens.

There was an abrupt end to the woman's rant when the person who was giving out the keys stormed in.

Holding her masks under her chin, she shouted, "Pipe down! What's the problem?" She walked to the front of the classroom and put her hands on her hips. "Who in the hell is complaining now?"

Oh boy.

The complainer sat down in her chair. "I just want to know how your housekeeper died."

"You want to know how our housekeeper died?" Esther asked, bending over so they were practically eye to eye. "You want to know how our housekeeper died? I'll tell you how he died. He suffered for three weeks in intensive care, three weeks! Some days we heard he was getting better, but last night everything stopped—his heart, his kidneys, his lungs, his brain. Everything just stopped! That's what Covid does. He died of Covid. What else do you want to know?"

"I still don't like it," the woman said softly, "and you and this man send people like us up there!"

Esther gave the complainer a piece of her mind that I found a little difficult to understand even though her masks were under her chin. If I were to boil her words down to a single message, it would be that either she and/or Jermaine are on the Covid units all night side by side with their housekeepers.

"Jermaine and I aren't sitting in our office down here playing dominoes," she said.

Whew, our generals are on the front lines after all.

Jermaine broke the spell, "You don't have to stay if you don't want to," he said, "but we hope you will." The complaining woman stood up, picked up her purse, and walked out. A man, who had been sitting next to her, followed her out, looking back at us with a shrug.

Jermaine asked for our attention and introduced us to Esther Wakes, the assistant manager of the 11:00 pm to 7:00 am shift. By now she had her masks stretched up and back around her face, tight as a drum.

Esther handed him a pile of papers and left the room.

Jermaine stood up and paced the floor, pretending to look through the papers.

"If there are more of you who feel as she did, you don't have to stay," he said. "I don't want anyone staying here against their will."

The room became very still, and despite the fact that the complaining woman had walked out, her voice and those bitter warnings lingered.

Waiting a few moments, he looked at each of us and then gave us the handouts.

"What I will teach you in the next few minutes could make the difference between life and death for you and your housekeeper," he said. Then he paused and studied our faces.

"Let me say that again."

There was no need to repeat it. We got it the first time.

The first handout was a sketch representing the three zones, or degrees, of Covid contamination.

The hot zone is an area fully contaminated with Covid—the Covid patient's room. An employee in this room, with or without the patient present, is at high risk for Covid contamination. Essentially the hot zone is where Covid is still bursting into song, spitting little Covids everywhere. Housekeepers clean the hot zone room. Furloughs are not allowed inside.

The warm zone is usually a five-foot-wide, three-foot-deep section of the floor immediately outside the Covid patient's room. The boundaries of this zone are

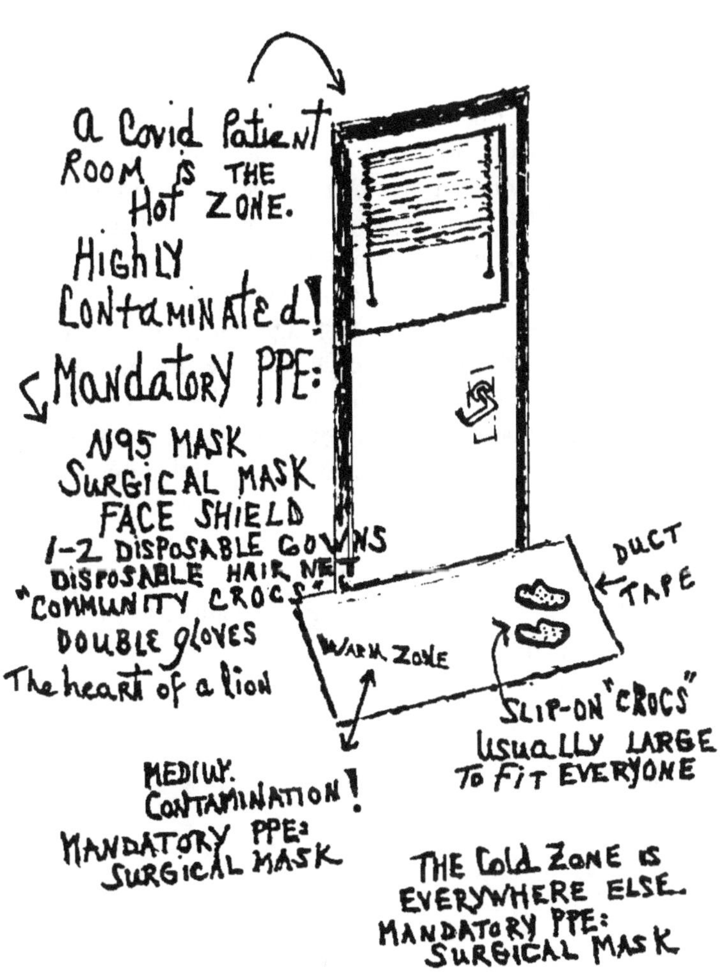
a Covid Patient
ROOM IS THE
Hot ZONE.
HighLY
Contaminated!
Mandatory PPE:
N95 MASK
SURGICAL MASK
FACE SHIELD
1-2 DISPOSABLE GOWNS
DISPOSABLE HAIR NET
"COMMUNITY CROCS"
DOUBLE gloves
The heart of a lion
DUCT
TAPE
WARM ZONE
SLIP-ON "CROCS"
usually LARGE
TO FIT EVERYONE
MEDIUM.
CONTAMINATION!
MANDATORY PPE:
SURGICAL MASK
THE Cold ZONE IS
EVERYWHERE ELSE.
MANDATORY PPE:
SURGICAL MASK

duct-taped and vary in size, with very large rooms having very large warm zones. Supposedly this warm zone is less contaminated than the hot zone. Furloughs are not allowed to step into this zone either.

All employees at Saints' love wearing Crocs, which are rubber, slip-on, indestructible shoes. Pairs of "community" Crocs of different sizes sit in the warm zone. Nurses and housekeepers remove their own shoes to slip into the "community" Crocs. Otherwise, Covid would hitchhike out of the hot zone and into the hallways attached to the employees' own shoes. Covid is a sneaky bugger.

The one zone that is furlough-friendly is the cold zone. The cold zone is everywhere the hot and warm zones are not. That covers a lot of territory. Is the cold zone contaminant-free? Is anywhere in the country contaminant-free? The answer is no. You just slap on a mask and hope for the best.

I ask the reader to forgive the accurate but messy illustration of the three zones on page 33.

By the way, the letters, PPE, stand for Personal Protective Equipment.

AUDREY AND SHANIA

It was only 12:30 am when Jermaine asked us to go to the cafeteria for lunch. For most women I know, the worst part of any new job is finding someone to have lunch with. I imagined everyone except me leaving the classroom holding hands and skipping merrily to the cafeteria. However, much to my relief, two women, Audrey and Shania, were also looking for lunch company.

Audrey, a tall, attractive woman in her thirties, is an administrative assistant in the corporate foundation center at Saints' Hospital. She was wearing a tight, stretchy white tunic, black leggings, and lace-up boots. Shania, a voluptuous twenty-something, is an ultrasound technician in the hospital's geriatric center. She was wearing a pink sweater set, matching short skirt, and cream-colored ankle boots.

With my voluptuous days behind me, I wore a loose black t-shirt, black jeans, and sneakers. My body image had suffered a serious blow during my great-nephew's recent fourth birthday party when one of his friends told me I resembled the yellow rubber chicken my great-nephew received that day as a present.

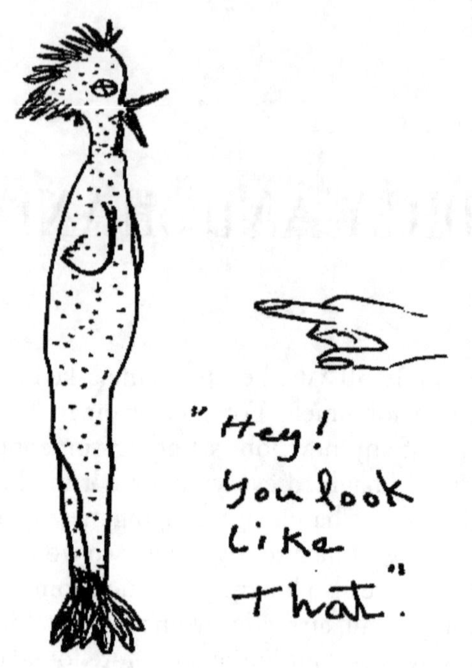

Being the last three to leave the classroom, we were approached by Jermaine, who offered to walk us to the cafeteria. Shania and Audrey had a lot to say along the way about Covid, reciting what they'd heard from the television and internet that day.

Then Shania told Jermaine she was sorry about his employee who died.

Audrey asked him, "If I catch Covid, do I have to use my own sick time?"

Jermaine thanked Shania for her sympathy and told Audrey that the State of NJ had financial provisions to provide for first responders' Covid sick time.

Before leaving, Jermaine reminded us to return to the classroom in an hour.

The cafeteria offerings were paltry: yogurt, wrapped cold-cut sandwiches, bananas, chips, and fried chicken. There was a hot beverage station and one refrigerator filled with cans of soda and iced tea.

The three of us bought fried chicken tenders and diet soda and picked a table not far from the cashier.

"Did you see how close the hot zone is to the warm and cold zones?" Audrey said while we were pulling our chairs out from under the table.

She continued, "And tell me, how does the bad Covid air stay inside the room once the door is opened?"

We sat down.

She continued, "Does Jermaine expect us to fall for that? He is just dishing out the best baloney the hospital bigwigs can come up with."

"Oh my God, you're right," Shania said. "I never thought of that."

"The zones are this close together," Audrey said holding her thumb and pointer finger an inch apart. "So, how is it possible," she continued, "that bad Covid air stays inside the patient's room when the door opens up? Somebody made this stuff up and is getting paid a lot of money for this."

"How could someone make money from this?" Shania asked Audrey.

"By getting us all killed," Audrey said loudly. The cashier turned around and looked at her.

I generally feel uncomfortable around crackpots and was about to excuse myself when Audrey redeemed herself.

"Well, I don't know why I said that. I'm sorry, that sounded crazy. I'm just upset."

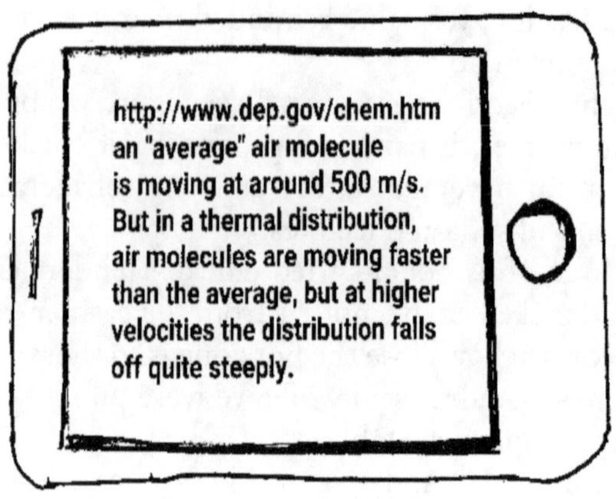

"If this is true," Audrey said, "we're goners."

We opened our containers of chicken and popped open our cans of soda.

Audrey continued, "But think about it. How can you keep bad air from mixing with good air? It's impossible. Anybody knows that air moves really fast."

"Well, how fast does air move anyway?" I asked.

This led us all to search the internet on our phones, where there were hundreds of sites that explained how different things—such as gases, solids, viruses, molecules, and air particles—travel at different speeds.

"This is ridiculous," Audrey said in disgust. "No wonder everybody hates science."

Finally, Shania came across one sentence we almost understood and read it to us, "An average air molecule is moving at around 500 m/s. That must be 500 miles per second."

This was sobering information.

"If this is true," Audrey said, "we're goners."

We all thought about that for a minute.

"And why are we picked for this?" Audrey asked. "Why are we the sacrificial lambs?" She leaned over the table, got close to us, and whispered, "He called Diane the lost lamb, didn't he?"

Shania's mouth dropped open.

I thought it was just a coincidence, although there was something disturbing about Jermaine's choice of the word lamb. But after his rough night, I didn't have the heart to find fault with him.

I said, "I think Jermaine isn't a bad guy. I mean, look at him. He's not going to send anyone to their doom. Really, look at him. He's so... so... nice."

"Maybe, maybe not," Audrey said.

After a lunch of fried chicken tenders topped with a few conspiracy theories, the three of us left the cafeteria and got lost.

We stopped employees and begged for directions, but all anybody knew was how to get to the hospital Starbucks from their own department. Starbucks was open 24/7.

Finally, a guy from the loading dock walked us up to Starbucks, where we called Jermaine, who sent Esther to get us.

It was after 3:00 am when Esther was finally able to retrieve us, and her hair, which had once been tied neatly into a bun, was now springing out in all directions.

"C'mon," she said grumpily.

"Wait, Esther." I said.

I asked Audrey and Shania for money. We rushed to put our few quarters together and bought Esther a mocha coffee. Shania used a contraption on her phone to buy her a lemon bar.

By the time we returned to the classroom, the other furloughs had gone home. We apologized to Jermaine for getting lost.

"Why didn't you use the electronic maps that are hanging on the walls?" he asked. "Do you know which ones I mean? They look like wide screen TVs, and they're everywhere!"

I nodded.

He continued, "I'm not being critical because I know this is all new for you ladies. All you need to do, ladies, is type in the letters EVS and it tells you where to go. If I can use them, anyone can—"

Audrey got a little heated and interrupted his fatherly blather. "We found lots of those map-things, Jermaine, and none of them worked. We were typing in EVS," she said, tapping her finger three times in the air, "and nothing came on the screen. I mean, we're not complete idiots!"

If my sixty-plus years have taught me anything, it's that I am a complete idiot.

"Where is everybody?" asked Shania, changing the subject.

"I let them go home after I taught them how to don, doff, and choke the swan," Jermaine said. "And as soon as I teach you these things, I'll send you home as well."

It was almost 3:30 in the morning, and Jermaine looked as neat as a pin. He wore a long-sleeve beige turtleneck without food stains, chestnut brown slacks without wrinkles, and polished black shoes without scuff marks.

"Now back to work," he said. We returned to our seats and looked at a handout. "First let me teach donning, doffing, and choking the swan."

"Your job as a furlough is to keep your housekeeper safe. Can you ladies repeat that?" We did.

He continued, "Every night each one of you will be paired with one of our most experienced housekeepers. You'll stay with them for their entire shift."

"When a Covid patient is transferred out of their room, Esther or I will contact your housekeeper to take care of that room by cleaning and sanitizing it."

Jermaine reiterated that we would be with their finest, most productive housekeepers who mean business.

Oh boy.

"Your job," he continued, "is to help your housekeeper put on their personal protective equipment, their

PPE, before entering the room. This is called donning. Then when they leave the room, you help them remove their PPE and sanitize it. This is called doffing.

"And furries," he said, bending over and looking into our faces.

"Yes," Shania said, leaning forward.

"You will help your housekeeper while you're in the cold zone. You are never to be in the warm or hot zones. Only the housekeeper can be in all the zones."

I was so confused.

We must have all looked baffled because Jermaine had us play-act donning and doffing. Everything was going okay until Shania pulled out some of Audrey's hair while removing her face shield. I thought Audrey contained her fury nicely.

after getting her hair pulled out, audrey contained her fury Nicely.

"I have a uniform for each of you," Jermaine said as he handed each of us a clear plastic bag with a charcoal gray uniform in it. "You have to wear this uniform to work. Never work in your own clothes."

"How did you know our size?" Shania asked.

"All the women get medium/large," he said. "You can go home now."

Audrey piped up, "What about choking the swan?"

"Geez," he said, clapping his hands and laughing. "I almost forgot!"

"While cleaning a room, housekeepers fill up lots of garbage bags that they will push out to you. Your job is to double bag each one, spin the top of the bag into a swan's neck. Then you simply tie the swan's neck into a knot and take the bag into the garbage room."

Jermaine said it was so simple that we didn't need to practice. Yeah. Right.

MAGNIFICENT MR. ABEO

THE NEXT NIGHT ESTHER PAIRED us up with an experienced housekeeper. I was the last furlough to be paired, so I thought I might not be needed when Esther informed a tall gentleman, Mr. Abeo, that his assignment tonight was the emergency room (ER) and that he would be taking me along.

I know I have seen people less happy to see me, but I can't remember when. He looked to be in his early thirties, more than six feet tall, and his uniform fit him like a glove. His pants were pressed and hemmed. His shirt was taken in a little at the sides. He was magnificent.

At the beginning of his shift, Esther had given Mr. Abeo the keys to his designated cart. The keys also opened some of the rooms that he might need access to. I followed him to his cart which he had already stocked with every supply imaginable. All the housekeepers kept their carts well stocked because returning to the department for something is a pain in the neck and wastes time.

"I'll push the cart," I said to him.

"You sure?"

"Oh, yeah," I said with enthusiasm, "I'm here to help you."

Mr. Abeo took off down the hall. I grabbed the handles and pushed. The cart didn't budge. Dammit. Checking to make sure he wasn't watching me, I turned around, pressed my shoulders against the handles, and it began to inch forward.

Mr. Abeo's legs were twice as long as mine, so keeping up with him was a problem for me. Soon it became apparent that it was a problem for him too because I lagged so far behind.

"Are you all right?" he'd ask after retracing his steps to find me.

"Yup," I'd say.

The third time he retraced his steps in search of a sexagenarian pushing a megalith was the last straw. He commandeered the cart.

During our lengthy and convoluted run to the ER, a troubling question preyed on my mind: Why am I racing through the corridors of a hospital in the middle of the night when other people my age are home asleep in bed grinding their teeth?

Most days, at least since I was fifteen years old, I have found myself in quasi-disasters. For example, I knocked down the New York City Macy's Christmas window exhibit in Manhattan when I reached in to feel the velvet skirt on a mannequin. Another time, while on a date, I took off my winter coat in a restaurant and saw that I had forgotten to put my skirt on. Chances are my life would have been much better spent—it certainly would have required less tidying up—if each morning I asked myself, "How can I prevent any problems today that may prevail upon me?"

We reached the double doors of the ER that automatically opened for Mr. Abeo, who charged through them like he was storming the Bastille. The ER was crowded with nurses, doctors, and housekeepers hurrying through the halls and in and out of rooms.

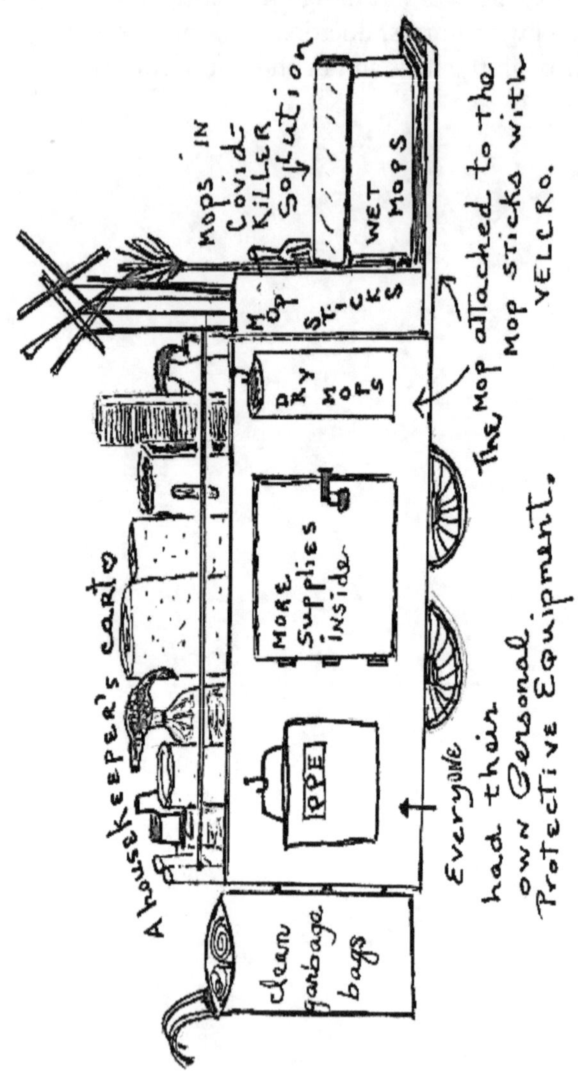
A housekeeper's cart
clean garbage bags
PPE
MORE Supplies INSIDE
DRY MOPS
MOP STICKS
WET MOPS
MOPS IN Covid-KILLER Solution
Everyone had their own Personal Protective Equipment.
The MOP attached to the MOP STICKS with VELCRO.

"I need to help another housekeeper over there," Mr. Abeo said, pointing to the other side of the ER. "Stay in this aisle, and push the cart down to the last room on the left. I'll meet you there in a couple minutes."

Squeezing the handles, I slowly pushed my way through the crowd, stopping constantly to let people pass in front of me. Doctors and nurses were huddled in the center of the aisle, talking quietly with each other about their patients who were suffering and dying in front of them. These were the early days of the pandemic. The death toll was mounting, and the snippets of conversations I heard were frantic:

"Why did his oxygen level drop so fast?"

"Did you call her family yet?"

"What's happening?... He was talking when he came in here."

"What about the woman in 2B? We have to hurry... vent... ICU?"

"She was fine an hour ago... gave her crackers... juice... then she's just... gone."

Oxygen levels in a Covid patient can drop faster than an anvil can drop from two feet above a floor. Unlike the straightforward trajectory of the anvil, Covid, for a few hours at least, will delay the oxygen from hitting bottom. Then, in an instant, Covid lets go, and the oxygen drops to zero.

I had hardly gotten ten feet when rushing toward me with a stretcher were two transport staff holding down a white sheet draped completely over a body. They stopped in front of my cart. "Move, move! Get out of the way!" I tried moving the cart backward and to the side. The housekeeping cart wouldn't budge.

"Get out of the way!"

"I'm trying!" I pulled the cart back a couple inches and tried pulling it to the side on an angle.

"Move it," one of them yelled.

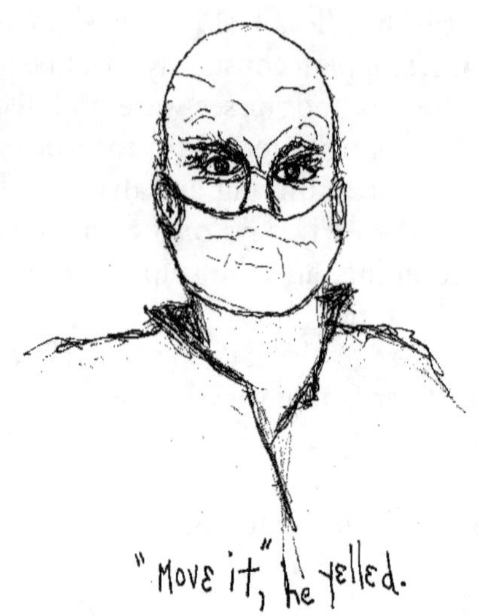

I stopped and looked at him. "I can't," I whispered under my mask. They backed up and pushed their way to the exit on the other side of the unit, everyone parting quickly as the stretcher went through.

"I'm suffocating," I whispered to Covid, who was behind me twisting a garrote around my neck.

Mr. Abeo finally showed up. "We need to get down there to that room."

I looked up at him. Every inch of me was soaked with sweat. I was melting. My surgical mask was wicking up tears.

"I know," he said kindly. "C'mon. We need to get down there."

He took the handle of the cart, pressing it through the crowd, apologizing as he went along. People opened the way for us, and after we passed, they refilled their places behind us.

The flimsy curtains that used to separate beds in the ER were replaced by makeshift walls with large windows for staff to watch their Covid patients carefully. A month earlier the patients in these rooms would have been on the side of the bed talking on their phone, turning around to ask their friend to get something out of the car. But the ill tonight were different—they were lying on their backs completely still, their chests puffed up like round loaves of bread.

We reached the room scheduled for cleaning. The patient had been out of the room for an hour. Technically Mr. Abeo should wait two hours for the room to "air out," but there were too many rooms to clean and too little time.

We were both standing in the cold zone when we commenced the quiet ritual of gowning up. I helped him on with his personal protective equipment:

- I tied a disposable gown for him in the back.
- I pulled double gloves up and over the sleeves of his gown.
- I handed him his N95 mask, which he put on and then layered a blue surgical mask over it.
- I sanitized his face shield and secured its placement.
- I gave him a disposable hair net, which he put on his head.
- I helped him remove his own shoes while he was in the cold zone and helped him keep his

> balance as he stepped into large "community" Crocs that were in the warm zone.

I then gave him some supplies from the cart, and he went inside the room and closed the door. With a surgeon's precision, he scrubbed and sanitized counters, chairs, the mattress, bed frame, phone, IV poles, the little knobs on the control panels behind the bed, areas on the wall that were covered in blood or other fluids, the door, and the windows that faced out into the aisle.

He opened the door a crack and squeezed out several garbage bags for me to double bag, spin into a swan's neck, and knot. I stuffed those bags into other bags and practically knocked myself out spinning the top of them into swan necks. I was taking a shot at choking one of the swans when Mr. Abeo cracked open the door and said, "Tumby tumper."

"What?" I asked.

"Tumby tumper," he said louder.

What? I had no idea what he said. Crap. I started sweating again, which made me nervous. Mr. Abeo made me nervous. Covid made me nervous. I was about to fake a heart attack when Mr. Abeo pulled his face masks down and calmly stated, "I need toilet paper."

It would have been easier for Mr. Abeo to stand on a ledge and catch a pigeon than to stretch over the warm zone to catch the roll of toilet paper I tossed.

Tossing TP to Mr. Abeo

A few minutes later he pushed out three more filled-up garbage bags, one with dirty linen. Pulling both face masks down, he spoke through the crack in the door, "I need clean linen." He was a little out of breath and had been in the room for more than forty-five minutes, and I wanted to get him out of there.

"Where's the linen room?" I asked.

"On the other side of the unit next to the medication room, which is the third door down on the right. Please hurry."

All the garbage bags he had previously pushed out for me to double bag and knot were still sitting there. He looked down at them and then at me.

"I can't choke the swan," I told him.

"What?"

"My gloves are sweaty and get stuck when I'm twisting the swan's neck so I can't choke it."

"Don't worry," he said tiredly. "I'll take care of it. Please get the linen."

I ran to the other side of the unit but couldn't remember where to go next.

I asked several employees to help me find the linen room, but that was to no avail. I had two options: I could run away or go back and tell Mr. Abeo that I cannot find the clean linen room. I was pondering how much incompetence one man could bear when an angel appeared in front of me.

"What's wrong, little lamb?"

"Jermaine!"

"You look lost."

"Thank God you are here, Jermaine." I hugged him awkwardly.

"Ah yes," he said backing up. "Are you lost again, little lamb?"

Several minutes later, while piling the linen onto my outstretched arms, Jermaine asked how things were going. I shrugged and nodded and shrugged again.

I now had a complete linen set:

- one fitted sheet
- one full sheet
- one half sheet to put under a patient in case the patient slides down in the bed and has to be pulled up
- one pillow
- one pillowcase
- one blanket

Mr. Abeo's head was sticking out of the door when I rounded the corner.

I handed him the clean linen.

After making the bed, he needed to mop the floor. He asked for a mop stick and three wet mop heads that had been soaking in Covid-killer solution. With great strength, he mopped until sweat poured down the sides of his face. As per protocol, while still inside the room, he pulled off his gloves and gown, putting both in a garbage bag. He stepped out of the room into the warm zone and gave me his face shield to sanitize. He stepped out of the "community" Crocs, and I helped him into his own shoes.

A few more times that night transporters roared by with a stretcher calling out for clearance. I pressed my body, face first, against the nearest wall. Most of the staff simply moved aside, lost in thought or conversation. We were in a war with Covid, a battle of attrition. Patients came into the ER and left shortly afterward covered on a stretcher. There was no way to tell if the poor soul on the stretcher had died or was still alive and being transferred to the intensive care unit or a Covid nursing unit upstairs. But as the science changed, the hospital policy changed. A couple weeks later only the Covid patients who had died were covered head to toe. Surviving patients were transferred through the halls wearing a mask and swaddled in a sheet with just their frightened eyes showing.

Mr. Abeo meticulously cleaned three more rooms in the ER that night, and he might have done more if he'd had an adept furlough. But what I lacked in ability I tried to make up for in genuine sweaty effort.

After finishing one room and heading to another, I asked him if he felt afraid of Covid.

"Of course. Anyone with a brain should feel afraid of Covid."

"Well, does it prey on your mind—"

He interrupted me. "Fear can keep people from moving. Some people cannot move from their houses. They stay inside. I cannot do that. I would feel like a prisoner."

"Well—"

He continued, "With every room I clean I think, 'This could be a neighbor or friend coming in next. It has to be safe for them.'"

I worked with many housekeepers during my weeks at the hospital and most said they were afraid of Covid but wouldn't let it immobilize them.

"Who knows, it could be my friend or family next in that room," they often told me.

Later that night, on our way to the fourth floor, I was surprised when Mr. Abeo abruptly stopped walking. I figured he was going to hand over the reins to me.

Instead he said, looking at me, "People think housekeepers are stupid."

"I don't," I said.

"People think we're stupid because all we do is clean up after them. They think I am stupid because they think this is all I am." He took hold of the cart, started walking, and continued, "My family in Africa have their own housekeepers, so I never tell them this is what I do in America. Maybe they think here I am someone important."

I looked up and watched his young face as he spoke and I wondered how often he suffers these thoughts. Few people would march through these halls every night risking their lives for others? I wanted to tell him what I was thinking, but I never did.

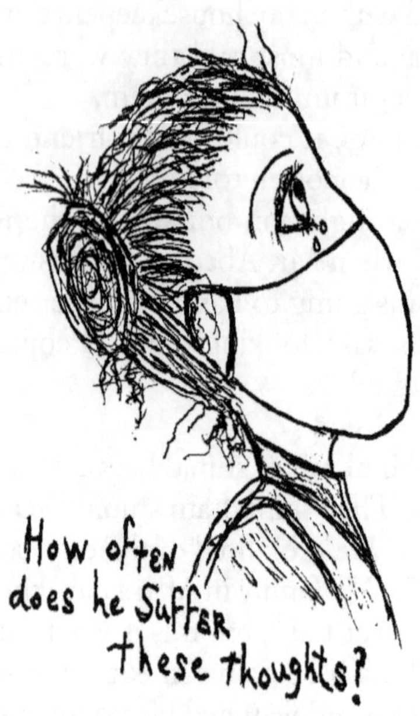

At 6:15 am, he and I headed back to the housekeeping department.

Mr. Abeo pushed the cart while I trotted alongside. After spending a long, exhausting night battling Covid together, a tacit trust united us. I had watched over him and he patiently did the same for me. His great heart kept me going.

He talked about his life back in Kenya and told me his father had twenty wives because his father is a wealthy plantain farmer. Being rich helps him keep all those wives entertained.

"How does he entertain them?" I asked.

"He has parties and buys them beautiful things."

"Don't all those women drive your dad crazy?"

"Why should they drive him crazy?" he asked. "They give him children and grandchildren. Let me think," he turned his head to the side, trying to remember something. "So far he has forty-two children and eight grandchildren."

I was trying to imagine the shape of his family tree and figured it looked more like a coat hanger.

"Are you the baby?" I asked.

He laughed. "You are a funny lady… very nervous, but funny." He pushed the cart into an elevator. "Why are you so nervous?"

"I'm not sure," I said honestly.

"You are more nervous… the most nervous… of anyone I have known," he said and pushed the ground floor button.

I watched the doors close and heard the bell for each floor we passed in our descent to the basement. I've always been a wreck, but I didn't know it was so obvious. The elevator doors opened. We stepped out into the hallway and continued this cringeworthy discussion.

"To be honest, Mr. Abeo, I think all this nervousness comes from my childhood when I grew up believing the Russians were going to yank me out from under my desk and sell me to the circus."

This is true. In grammar school, when most kids were daydreaming about kid stuff, I was daydreaming about building a nuclear shelter in my backyard.

"If you think about it," I said to him, "my whole generation is a little dotty."

"Listen, seriously," he said. He stopped walking and put his hand on my shoulder. "You should not be nervous. You are old now and should be wise."

It was hard to argue with that.

NURSES

For weeks the pandemic surge continued. An unfortunate policy in this hospital, imposed early in the surge, demanded that only a registered nurse (RN,) doctor, physician assistant, or nurse practitioner were allowed inside Covid patients' rooms.

RNs had to limit their visits with Covid patients to no more than 20 minutes. This was impossible. These RNs were dancing as fast as they could, giving their patients medication, feeding and toileting them, changing intravenous solutions, and holding cell phones and iPads for families to see their loved ones. Caring for these suffering patients inevitably took more than 20 minutes.

The certified nursing assistants (CNAs,) who provide invaluable support to the nurses, were not allowed to be in the patient rooms with the nurses.

The CNAs had the same job with their nurses that we had with our housekeepers: stay in the cold zone and keep their nurses safe. However, some nights there were not enough nursing assistants to help the RNs, so furloughs would be asked by a busy RN to assist him or her. We would don and doff for the nurse and then run between two rooms, helping both the nurse and our housekeeper. The hospital was bursting at the seams with Covid patients, so running between two rooms was happening more often.

At our 3:00 am lunch, Shania, Audrey, and I expressed concern about this situation because it extended the time our housekeepers were left in the hot zone. However, the housekeepers never complained and told us to share our supplies with the nurses if they needed them.

Fortunately, the policy of only RNs or doctors allowed in the patients' rooms was changed, and nursing assistants were allowed to enter the rooms to assist the RNs in the care of the patients.

When a patient passed away, the nurse would call for a physician to confirm the patient's death. Once the patient's death was confirmed, the nurse would place the patient in the body bag and prepare the deceased for transport to the morgue. If the physician was unable to call the patient's family, it was the nurse who would make the call.

I remember seeing an RN caring for an elderly, dying patient who was able to tell her that he loved Frank Sinatra. She put her cell phone next to him on his pillow and he was lulled to eternal sleep with his favorite music. She cried a lot after he died. The other staff gave her a few moments of comfort, but there was no time for meaningful sympathy. Covid was circling overhead. This was no time to stop.

After a month there was another change that helped the nurses. The patients' medications began to be provided from medication carts placed outside the patients' doors. This included intravenous solutions that contained much of the patients' medications. These solutions were delivered to every patient through a long infusion tube that traveled safely to the patient. This significantly reduced the time the RNs spent in the hot zone. It also helped them predict when the solution would run out so there was no interruption in medication management.

My own exposure to Covid felt inevitable. I worried about contracting Covid as I drove home every morning after work.

Imagine this ugly scenario: You've worked a long shift in the hospital. You finally get into your car to go home. You turn the key, shift into reverse, and look into the rearview mirror. But instead of seeing what you usually see in the rearview mirror, you see lots of little Covids on your head jumping up and down, waving at your reflection.

So, I designed a Covid-killing, "keep the bugger inside the hospital" routine for myself:

> 6:45 am—Before my shift is over, I fetch the clean laundry bag from Jermaine's office that I had brought from home. Inside the laundry bag are my clean clothes and shoes.
>
> 6:50am - Squeezing into one of the narrow ladies' room stalls, I change out of my dirty uniform, including my shoes and socks, and stuff them into the laundry bag. Then I change into the clean clothes I brought from home.
>
> Inside that skinny bathroom stall, I ricocheted off the walls and door as I changed clothes. It became a cross my body had to bear.
>
> 7:10 am—I walk to my car in the hospital employee parking lot, throw the laundry bag into the trunk, and cover my driver's seat with a clean bedsheet I brought from home.
>
> 7:50 am— After reaching home, I step out of my car and slip into clean shoes that I placed next to my parking spot last night before heading out to work.
>
> After smushing the shoes I wore in the car, the bedsheet, and my coat into the laundry bag, I head up to our apartment.

> 7:55 am- I drag myself and that wretched laundry bag into the bathroom and take a hot shower.
>
> 8:10 am – Before going to sleep, I pass by the laundry room and put every piece of contaminated clothing, the sheet, and the laundry bag into the wash.
>
> 10:15 pm—Drive back to work in my clean uniform with the clean, full laundry bag and bedsheet in the trunk.

Repeat above 30 times.

I cried only once at home, and that was in the shower. I had just come off a shift where the housekeeper and I were assigned to the intensive care unit. The nurses told us that for the past week in their unit not one patient lived for more than twenty-four hours. The nurses were matter-of-fact about telling us. We were matter-of-fact about hearing it.

NADYA THE FORMIDABLE

IT WAS A LITTLE AFTER 3:00 am on a Sunday and Shania, Audrey, and I were having our usual lunch of fried chicken tenders. Shania was talking about a housekeeper, Nadya, with whom she was paired last night.

"I heard she is great," I said.

"Well, —" Shania started.

Then I interrupted her with, "I heard she has one of those razors that scrape the gunk out of the cracks where the walls and floor meet."

Audrey nodded her head in appreciation.

"Well," Shania said louder, "Nadya is terrifying! She told me to go to the kitchen and get her a gallon of a sanitizer called Right-Oh. She even spelled it out for me."

"Is it any good?" Audrey asked.

"Just wait," Shania was annoyed with all the interruptions. She continued, "So I went down to the kitchen and asked the chef for Right-Oh, and she said that there's no such thing as Right-Oh, and I was the third furlough from housekeeping that week asking her for something she'd never heard of."

"You were ditched," I said surprised. "What did you do?"

But Audrey and I knew the answer. Shania did what every ditched furlough usually does. Go to Starbucks, buy coffee and a lemon bar, and spend the rest of the night in an empty closet or abandoned exam room scrolling through their phone.

As luck would have it, I was paired with Nadya the next night.

It was Monday night, a little before 11:00 pm. There was confusion in the housekeeping corridor because the metal case holding all the housekeepers' keys was missing.

Esther was running from room to room looking for it. She finally found it under a pile of pizza boxes, lugged it to the front of the line, and dropped it on the table with a bang.

Nadya, always first in line, was vexed by the delay. With Covid breathing down everyone's neck, tensions were high, and tempers flared without much provocation.

Already at the end of her rope, Esther saw me standing nearby and barked at me to follow Nadya.

Following Nadya to her cart, I offered to push, but she took hold of it and sped off. In her forties now, she had emigrated to the United States from Russia at twenty. A little under five feet tall, Nadya had a muscular figure that reminded me of a bowling pin turned upside down. I was a bit wary around her because I had spent some time in Russia and never met a Russian who suffered fools gladly.

I was jogging to keep up with her when she stopped in front of a set of elevators. A door opened, and Nadya rushed in with the cart, waving goodbye to me as the doors closed. It was 11:10 pm and I was ditched already. Crap. This must be a record even for Nadya.

A ditchee never goes back to Esther or Jermaine to complain about it. These housekeepers are the hardest working people we ever knew and dragging around a mind-numbing furlough all night cannot be easy.

I had $5.00 with me, but I didn't feel like going to Starbucks. I figured I would go to the ER and help empty garbage cans. A set of elevator doors opened. Nadya was there with her hands on her hips, tapping her right foot. I got into the elevator.

Nadya generally takes care of the two large Covid units on the third floor. The turnover there was rapid because people were either being transferred to the intensive care unit (ICU) or, sadly, passing away.

Refusing to follow the housekeeping protocol of waiting two hours for rooms to be aired out before cleaning, Nadya started to clean as soon as we got there. She said this was not the time to stand on protocol.

I helped her don her PPE. She double gowned, which meant that she put the first gown on like a coat and tied the bow in front of her. Then I helped her on with the second gown, which I tied behind her. Donning, as always, was serious business. The units were especially quiet tonight with staff being helped on and off with PPE.

Nadia wore the N95 mask with a blue surgical mask over it and a face shield over that. We were in the cold zone when I helped her off with her shoes and then I held on to her when she slipped into the warm-zone Crocs. Her bowling pin shape interfered with her balance, but we managed. While she stood in the warm zone, I handed her what she asked for from her housekeeping cart. Then she went into the room. Covid had no defense against her.

I noticed a bent-over, heavyset nurse in bright blue scrubs shuffling toward me. She reached our room, sprinkled baby powder on the floor under the door, and we both watched as every speck of baby powder disappeared instantly into the room. She put her hand on her lower back and straightened up.

"Oh my God," she said, "my back is killing me."

"Do you want me to massage it a little for you," I offered.

"Now aren't you just the sweetest thing?" She arched her spine backward.

"Did my back just crack?"

"I think so."

"I'm getting too old for this," she said, leaning both arms on the housekeeping cart.

Nadya cracked the door open and asked for more wipes. I gave her the wipes.

"And more paper towels please," she said quietly.

I gave her what she wanted, and she went back inside.

"What are you doing?" I asked the nurse while she arched her back again.

She swung herself upright.

"Just making sure the machines are working," she said, pointing into the room. "See that big thing in there… the thing that looks like a silver caterpillar? Look inside the room," she said pointing to the window in the door. "C'mon, it's not going to come through the window and bite you!"

Looking that closely into the room required that I stand in the warm zone, which made me queasy.

"Go ahead and look," she said impatiently. "I haven't got all night."

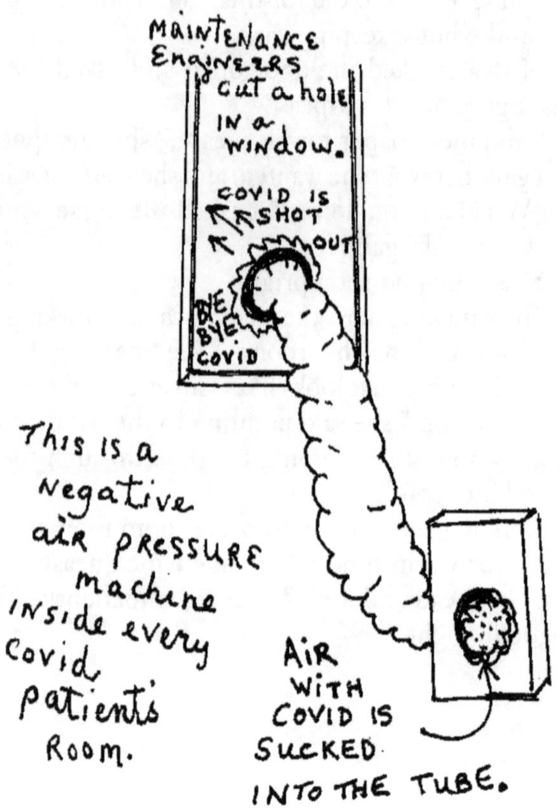

I stepped into the warm zone and looked through the window.

"Do you see that big tube in the room? Do you see it? It's big as life, and you're blind as a bat if you can't see it."

"Yeah, I see it," I said. It looked like a ten-foot-long wrinkled caterpillar tube wrapped in aluminum foil, hanging halfway in and halfway out of a hole in one of the windows.

"Every minute that thing is sucking Covid out of the room," she said proudly. "That thing is a giant vacuum sucking in Covid air and sending it out into the great beyond."

I imagined little Covids hanging onto a toilet seat by their fingernails, only to get sucked, one by one, into caterpillar hell.

The nurse was swinging her arms in a wide arc. "All that air leaving a room creates negative air pressure. It reduces the pressure of the air in the room so the bad stuff can get sucked out of the room. It helps to keep Covid from escaping out the door when the door has to be opened," she said, yawning.

Well slap me silly, I thought. Jermaine wasn't lying when he said the warm zone wasn't as contaminated as the hot zone.

"This baby powder is like the canary in the mine," she continued, waving the container around. "Sprinkling it under the closed door tells me whether or not the tubes are working." She pointed to the floor under the door in front of us. "I know that tube in there is working cause if it wasn't the baby powder would still be sitting there."

"How does good air get in?" I asked.

"See the things up in the ceiling in the patient's room? Those are vents that are constantly pushing clean, fresh air into the room."

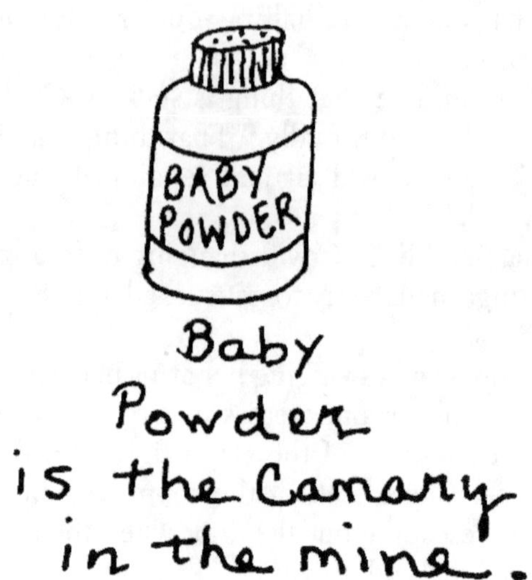

She stretched her back once more before she shuffled down the hall and found a room where the baby powder stayed in a little pile under the patient's door. Pulling a phone out of her pocket, she made a call, and a few minutes later a couple of burly guys arrived, geared up, went inside the room, and slapped that caterpillar back into action.

I read later that while the hospitals were filling up with dozens of Covid patients every day, there was no time to order fancy negative air pressure systems. The building services and engineering departments in hospitals designed and built these contraptions in record time, usually buying parts from local hardware stores.

All was going well until Nadya cracked the door open and asked me to get her something. Behind two masks and a face shield she said something like, "Oh lala layna."

"What?" I asked.

"Oh lala layna," she said louder.

"What?" I repeated.

"Oh… lala… layna," she roared.

Oh boy.

Hot sweat rolled out of sweat glands I never knew I had. I pointed to everything in the cart. "Is it this?" I asked. "Or this, or that, or… ?" Maybe I could pretend to faint.

She pulled her masks down and hollered, "I need toilet paper!"

"But you said you needed something like lala luna," I meekly replied.

She shrugged, and I got her toilet paper.

I helped her clean a few more rooms. It was 3:00 am, and I told her it was time for my lunch.

"Me too," she said pointing to a set of double doors. "I will meet you there at 4:00 am. Do not be late."

COVID AND THE SINGLE LIFE

SHANIA AND AUDREY WERE ALREADY eating when I sat down and told them I was working with Nadya that night.

"Did she get mad at you or try to ditch you?" Shania asked.

"I think she was going to ditch me and changed her mind."

"I'm with Mr. Abeo tonight," Audrey said, batting her eyelashes. "Do you think he has a girlfriend?"

"I don't know. I never met him," Shania said.

"Do you think I should ask him out?" Audrey asked me.

"Sure, why not," I said, squirting ketchup on my chicken.

"Did he tell you that his dad has twenty wives?" Audrey asked.

"Yeah," I said.

"You believe him?"

"Yeah," I said.

"I don't. I can't believe you fell for that crapola," Audrey chided.

Shania said, "I think that is so interesting. Let's say his father does have twenty wives and each wife has two babies. Then Mr. Abeo would have forty brothers and sisters."

"Thirty-nine," Audrey corrected.

Shania looked at Audrey. "Ask him if he's the baby."

When we have lunch, the cafeteria is usually deserted except for three consistent people: the chef, the cashier, and the same employee who sits in a booth sound asleep.

On a card table next to the cashier was a pyramid of toilet paper. Each roll cost a dollar. I was reflecting on the scarcity of toilet paper when Audrey said she doesn't need much toilet paper because she is single and lives alone.

"I'm lonely," Audrey said. "I used to have a social life, and now I just sit in my apartment alone." She was drinking her diet soda with a straw and started blowing bubbles in the bottom of the can. She looked up from her straw. "I think I'm going to try one of those dating sites. You know, they're still up and running."

"Have you done that before?" Shania asked, chewing with her mouth open.

"Yeah. I met a guy who was okay. We went out for a while."

"What happened to him?" Shania asked.

"I broke up with him. If I had known Covid was coming, I wouldn't have broken up with him."

"If you're interested in Mr. Abeo, ask him if he wants to go to Starbucks for coffee," I suggested.

"Starbucks? Upstairs? We can't sit in there, you know that."

"Take the coffee to go," I told her.

"Where would we go after that - sit in a mop closet?"

"Bring him here to the cafeteria," said Shania. After a few moments she added, "I want to go on those dating sites, but my parents won't let me."

"Shania, how old are you?" Audrey asked.

"Twenty three and—"

Audrey interrupted, "Your parents can't tell you what to do. Once you're eighteen, you can do whatever you want."

"Well, I live with them and I just don't… you know… well, I don't know…"

Audrey was getting impassioned—which usually meant she was about to say something that would embarrass herself, someone else, or both. "Let me ask you, Shania, in confidence, are you a virgin?"

I stopped drinking my soda and looked inside the can. "It's not every day, Shania, that somebody asks you if you're a virgin," I said.

"I don't really want… to… say…"

"It's okay," Audrey said, "you don't have to tell me if you don't want to. I'm just being honest here." She picked up one of her chicken tenders, dipped it into barbecue sauce and pointed the chicken at Shania. "I've got to get you out of your parents' house." A glob of BBQ sauce dripped onto the table. "After Covid," she was wagging the chicken tender at Shania, "I'll teach you a couple things, and then we'll go out to a Latin club and meet some of those men who know how to dance."

"Covid might last forever," Shania pointed out.

"Then I'm doing myself in," Audrey stated.

Audrey would be the last person to do herself in. She loves an audience, and unless she befriends a psychopath, no one will let her kill herself while they're standing close by.

"Girls," Audrey leaned over and whispered, "I cannot live forever without... s... e... x."

Whenever I hear the word "sex," I think of my Irish roots and the family I had growing up. The word was never mentioned in our house, and, what's worse, every adult with whom I shared even a speck of DNA went out of their way to stymie my comprehension of it completely.

"When I was eleven," I told them, "my great Aunt Judy Ruth told me that a baby is born after a mom and dad sit side by side twice on a couch."

IRISH SEX EDUCATION:

A baby is BORN afTER a mom and dad sit side by side twice ON a couch.

Audrey laughed and spit out a little of her soda.

"And then," I kept on, "you guys will never believe this, but when I was in eighth grade, I still didn't know anything about sex."

"I believe it," Audrey said. "Your generation was a little slow in that department."

"But I had a friend," I went on to say, "who was Italian—"

Audrey interrupted, "Italians know everything about sex. It's in their genes. I read that."

"Well, I asked my Italian friend if I could have sex with my underpants on. And do you know what she said? She said I could have sex with my underpants on, but only if they had a hole in them."

Audrey spit out a little more of her soda.

Relating this story makes me uncomfortable, and this was only the second time that I mentioned it in public. The first was four decades ago at an elegant wedding reception where my married, very pregnant sister volunteered to be my date. Standing on a wraparound porch watching the Atlantic Ocean, I complimented her on the powder blue linen sheath she was wearing.

Flittering by in a little black bow tie outfit was a young waitress carrying a tray of champagne flutes in one hand and a bottle of champagne in the other.

"Keep them coming," I said, lifting a flute off her tray.

"I will," she said with a little laugh while pouring champagne into my flute. Thankfully, she proved herself to be a woman true to her word.

My sister was talking about her last-minute decorating plans for the baby's room when a tall woman, one of the guests from the bride's side of the family, appeared in front of us.

"You're very sparkly," I said.

She laughed and told us she loved diamonds but wasn't a snob about it but that her family "was in jewelry" and that she wore her diamonds only at special events "like this beautiful reception."

She was a gabber, which we appreciated because my sister and I tend to be shy with strangers. When we first got to the reception, I had asked my sister if she wanted to "work the room." But much to my relief, she said she'd rather put pins in her eyes.

My reliable young bow-tied friend showed up again, handing Sparkly a glass of champagne, swapping my old glass with a new one, and then flittering away.

"I do like your earrings," I said to Sparkly. "They have little holes in them."

"They are not holes," Sparkly said. "In our trade we call them chandelier earrings, and the little openings help the light to shine through." She gave an annoyed shake of her head and repeated, "They are definitely not holes."

"Holes… that reminds me of a story," I said and proceeded to tell her about the hole in the underpants.

After Sparkly left in disgust, my sister and I watched the ocean waves for a few quiet moments.

"Whatever possessed you to tell that story?" my sister asked, looking up at me.

"I don't know," I said looking down at her. "Let's get some food."

After lunch, promptly at 4:00 am, I met Nadya by the double doors of her two Covid units. We had cleaned a few rooms on the one unit, and now we were going to the other.

"We are running short on time," she said. "You need to move faster. You need to pay attention to get what I need!" She snapped her fingers.

I nodded. I might be able to obey her commands. Every housekeeper has a unique cleaning routine, so furloughs can usually predict what their housekeeper will need next. It helped that the doors to patients' rooms had a window so I could see when Nadya was running out of something.

For example, Nadya always dry-mops a floor before wet-mopping. Not everyone does that. She sweeps the floor with the dry mop head that picks up lint and light debris. When that's done, she opens the door and hands me the dry mop. Then I give her the wet mop that has been soaking in the Covid-killing solution.

She was nearing the end of cleaning a room when she opened the door, tossed out the bag of dirty linen, and closed the door. This was her signal that she was ready to make the bed and needed clean linen.

We were at the tail end of a long hall of patient rooms. On this particular unit, the patient rooms are on one side of the hall. The other side of the hall are rooms for staff supplies, such as the medication room, oxygen room, garbage room, restroom, and infusion supplies. In the middle is the nurses' station. Walking slowly up the hall, I read the sign on each door that I passed, but there was no linen room.

Halfway up the hall I stopped at the nurses' station. "Where is the linen room?" I asked.

They didn't answer me. I kept walking and passed a few more rooms, but none had the sign for linen.

"Do you know where the linen room is?" I asked a nursing assistant walking by pushing a cart.

"Don't know," he said and kept walking.

I returned to the nurses' station, where a unit clerk had just arrived with coffee.

"Where is the linen room?" I asked.

"I don't know."

"How is it possible that no one knows where the linen room is?" I asked.

A loud ruckus started at the far end of the hall where Nadya was still working. I saw her outside of the room banging the end of the mop stick on the floor hollering for me to come back. Bang! Bang! Bang! Bang!

a Loud Ruckus started down the hall. It was Nadya banging the end of the mop stick on the floor.

I grabbed the unit clerk's arm. "I need to know where the linen room is," I pleaded, tightening my hold on her arm.

"Let go of me!"

"You don't understand," I said to her, breathless, still squeezing her arm. "Do you see that woman down there banging the mop on the floor?"

She leaned over and looked, "Yeah. So?"

"You see her," I said practically spitting. "Well, if I don't bring her clean linen she's going to kill me." I motioned with my hand slitting my throat.

The unit clerk yanked her arm out of my grip and walked to the other side of the nurses' station.

I walked slowly to Nadya, who was still banging the mop on the floor, now surrounded by a small crowd. I could hear her repeating the word stupid.

I stood in front of her. "I can't find the linen room."

She picked up the mop handle and, just missing my head, pointed across the hall to the door that read, "Oxygen."

"That's not the linen room," I said pointing to the sign on the door. "It says Oxygen!"

She waved the mop stick side to side, still pointing at the door. "Oxygen," I said to her again.

"Open the door," she commanded. I did. It was the linen room. I got her the clean linen.

Following the debacle with the linen, Nadya and I didn't speak to each other for the rest of the night. Marching from room to room with frequent "harumphs," she made it plain that this would likely be the end of our short time together. This unswerving resolve to flush incompetence from her path kept her at the top of her

Covid-killing game. When Covid saw Nadya coming down the hall, he gasped and ran for cover.

Time dragged that night, but finally it was a little after 6:30 am and we were leaving our last Covid room to go back to the housekeeping department. Not wanting to end our shift on a sour note, I thought I'd offer her a sincere compliment.

"I like the way you make the patients' beds. You are very precise, and they look inviting."

"What do you mean inviting?"

"They look… like a wonderful place to get a good night's sleep."

"Thank you," Nadya said. "A patient wants a clean, comfortable bed. Right?"

"Absolutely right," I said.

"When I am sick," she continued, "I do not want to get into a bed that is dirty with crumbs. It would make me feel worse. Right?"

I agreed.

"We are here to help patients feel good and get better and go home. That is why we are here. Right?"

I nodded my head vigorously.

"If we do not make the beds, a patient will get into a bed that is sticky and smells like an old turkey," she said.

"Nadya, maybe the patient would like the bed if it smelled like a baby turkey instead of an old turkey," I said, thinking that would crack her up.

She turned around and squinted her small eyes. "So, you think you are funny, huh? You like making jokes? I hear you. You think it is good to be funny in this hospital? Follow me."

Nadya walked back to the Covid unit we had just left. She entered the unit and pointed at a patient's room. "Look in there."

The patient was an elderly man who was clearly dying. A nurse was holding up an iPad in front of him. I imagined his family looking at him and saying goodbye.

Nadya looked up at me, "You want to go in there and tell the patient your funny joke? Huh?"

Oh boy.

"Well, would you?" she asked again, her hands on her hips.

"Of course not."

"Everything is funny to you, right? Tell him your joke. Go ahead." She pushed her chin out pointing to the patient's door. "Go ahead, go, open the door, tell your joke."

She harumphed and left. I followed her to a housekeeping closet and waited while she parked her cart.

"I'm sorry," I said to her. "I'm very sorry, Nadya."

She straightened some of the cleaning supplies on the top of her cart and walked out of the closet, nearly knocking me over.

Nadya was right. I was ashamed and deserved that kick in the head. I called in sick the next night. I wasn't sick, but I had a lot to think about.

AHTI AND THE FINNS

Marriage to a seamstress for forty-five years had earned Ahti a uniform so perfect it could probably walk around on its own.

With a round face, wide neck, wide shoulders, no waist, short solid legs, and flat feet, Ahti reminded me of every man on my husband's side of the family.

It was the beginning of our shift, and I followed him to his cart, which was not where he had left it.

"This is the story of my life," he said, sighing.

I followed him into the storeroom, where he found his cart behind a skyscraper of toilet paper. It was stuck between the flatbed holding the toilet paper and the cinder block wall.

"It's the story of my life," he said, shaking his head. "Nothing is easy."

"Let me get someone to help," I said.

"No, no," he said looking up at the ceiling. "I can do it."

He yanked the cart backward so violently that it came out on the two back wheels, nearly flipping over onto him. This says a lot about Ahti's physical condition as the carts weigh hundreds of pounds and are at least five feet long.

"That was amazing, Ahti! How did you do that?"

There was a long litany of sighs as he ignored my question and looked through the cart. "I put toilet paper rolls inside here yesterday, and, of course, they're gone."

Alas, this was a problem that could be quickly remedied, but I could tell it weighed heavy on his heart.

Ahti is a man who finds the world a great disappointment. And because he expects constant disappointment, he has nothing to look forward to. He is from Finland. I know the Finns are some of the happiest people on earth, but I do find that some can be quite gloomy.

My husband is Finnish and can be gloomy. He says some Finns are that way because their ancestors lived through 600 years of invasions by just about anybody who had a boat, a horse, or a good pair of skis.

"We're not gloomy, we're stoic," my husband says. "Just imagine if your village was pillaged every time you turned around."

Then he dreams up a scene in a Finnish village from his ancestral past: His great, great, great grandmother is sitting at a table with her husband. She made some nice lutefisk for him because he worked a long day.

After they are seated at the dinner table, the husband says, "The village was pillaged this morning. They stole the pigs, burned down the church, everybody's alive, but they're all down a well."

His wife nods and says, "Pass the lutefisk."

The housekeepers all complain a lot about Ahti because he refuses to clean Covid. Instead, he is assigned to the medical office suites in a part of the hospital that are hardly used.

This Covid-free cleaning tonight with Ahti was a welcome change for me. I didn't even mind the mind-numbing slog to the other side of the hospital. We were about to enter a medical office suite when Ahti's work phone rang. With Ahti's phone to his ear, I could hear Jermaine telling him that an operating room (OR) on the floor below the ER had to be cleaned after a Covid patient had emergency surgery.

"No," Ahti said and hung up.

Jermaine called back, repeating what he had just said.

Ahti hung up again and said to me, "I'm not cleaning Covid."

Jermaine called back, so I took the phone. "I will do it. I know what to do," I said.

"Little lamb, you cannot go into contaminated rooms," Jermaine said. "I expect Ahti to do what every housekeeper here is expected to do. I need Ahti to take care of that OR. I have no one else tonight who has the time to take care of it."

I looked at Ahti, whose hands were in a prayer position as he looked up at the ceiling. Then he whispered, "I have no PPE."

Poor ole Jermaine blew a fuse, "I heard that, Ahti! You know that every one of you has PPE. We fit every employee with PPE. Ahti, you have PPE. I know you have PPE… blah blah… PPE… blah blah… PPE…"

I looked at Ahti, who now had his hand positioned like a gun to his head.

Jermaine continued, "He has PPE. I gave it to him myself. It must be in his locker."

"Oh Jermaine, wow, Ahti just said he'll do it. We're going to get his PPE now," I said and hung up.

"We have to go to your locker now and get the PPE," I said as kindly as I could. He needed his fitted N95 mask and face shield. It took us twenty minutes to get to Ahti's locker. He opened it, and what did we find? His coat and an old banana. He threw the banana in the trash and closed the locker door.

"See?" he said. "No PPE. I never got PPE."

"Let's go to the office and get some."

"No, I can't," Ahti said. "Jermaine will get so angry. Maybe we can get PPE while we're near the ER."

"Good thinking, Ahti," I said, and we force-marched our way back to the ER. As soon as we got there, I tracked down the charge nurse and asked if she would give Ahti some PPE for cleaning the OR.

She looked me up and down and said, "You people have your own PPE."

"You people have your own PPE," the ER charge nurse said.

Call me paranoid, but that felt personal.

Ahti gently took my arm and walked me out of the ER.

"She was right, Ahti," I said. "Why would anyone trust me enough to give me anything? Look at me."

He did and sighed. My uniform was too big for me. I never ironed it, and the pant legs dragged on the floor.

"Let's go back to the office, Ahti, and ask Jermaine for some PPE."

"No, no, no," he said with a small grin, wagging his finger.

"I don't want to give up, Ahti."

"But now is the best time to give up," he said. He took my elbow, and we walked away.

After much pleading, Ahti finally agreed to do the job. I think it helped that I told him I would clean the operating room with him. We took the elevator down one floor, stepped out of it, and— no surprise—walked into a massive construction site. Following laminated signs pointing to the OR, we zigzagged our way through partition walls that had an uncanny resemblance to a corn maze. After several turns, we arrived at the cardiac catheterization recovery room, which also served as a dead end. Ahti commenced a litany of sighs.

"Let's just go the other way," I said.

He turned the cart around, and we made our way back to the elevator.

"Have you been down here before?" I asked him.

"Not since they started doing construction," Ahti replied.

We walked past the elevator, and after a few short turns we were standing in front of the double glass doors of the operating room.

"At last!" exclaimed a nurse hurrying up to us with her arms waving. "The marines have landed, and they're here to clean our operating room!"

I haven't seen anyone this excited since we got the news from the government in March that the pandemic was over.

She stopped waving her arms when she noticed we were not wearing any PPE except for a couple of skimpy surgical masks.

"Where's your PPE?" she asked.

Ugh. Here we go again. But, alas, this nurse was not only forgiving, she was unstoppable.

"No PPE? No problem! Come right this way," she sang as she led us into a long, skinny room with floor-to-ceiling shelves stuffed with PPE: booties to put over our shoes, gowns, gloves, goggles, face shields, every type of mask imaginable, clear garbage bags, red hazard bags, hand sanitizer, wipes, and the biggest box of Russell Stover candy I ever saw.

"I never saw a box of candy that big," I said.

She lifted it off a shelf, placing it on a wobbly metal cart. "It's ten pounds—a gift from my mother."

She opened the box and held the lid up in the air as we all peered down into the vast sea of chocolate.

"What'dya want?" she asked.

"What'dya want, Ahti?" I asked.

"How can I tell them apart?" he asked.

After pointing out to Ahti the identities of the wee chocolates from the chart inside the box, we all put on gloves, plucked out four chocolates each, and stood together in a small circle eating them.

The nurse's identification badge said her name was "Pranauthi" but she told us to call her Prana. In her thirties, Prana had thick, dark hair twisted into a braid so long it reached her waist. Her eyes were the color of her scrubs, and her scrubs were the color of the blue turquoise stones she wore around her neck. Ahti couldn't take his eyes off her, except once when he went back to get more chocolate.

"See this?" she said, pointing to the shelves. "Not only will I provide you guys with protective equipment, I'll give you doubles of everything. Plus," she said conspiratorially, "I even have two nice drawstring bags. I'll fill each one with PPE and put your name on your bag. Hang them on your housekeeping cart." Every housekeeper except Ahti had their PPE in one of those bags hanging somewhere on their cart.

Prana piled gowns, face shields, etc., on a small, rickety trolley, and we followed her to the operating room double doors. Ahti and I stood in the cold zone while Prana methodically helped us on with all our gear. We stood there like kids while Prana gowned us up and checked that everything fit securely. There were no "community" Crocs for us to wear, so she helped each of us into double paper booties.

During my furlough at Saints, with the exceptions of Jermaine and Mr. Abeo, no one took the time to care about me. Well, really, who could blame them? Would you stop running if you had a target on your back?

"So, you two dears, which one of you will be staying out here with the housekeeping cart?" Prana asked, pulling up the second set of gloves over the sleeves of Ahti's gown.

"We're both going inside," I said. "It's such a big room. We'll be fine."

I was relieved that she didn't object. The protocol for donning and doffing made it clear that once inside the room, the housekeeper was not to return to the cart but to rely on the furlough for whatever they needed. And one more thing: The housekeeping cart was never, ever to go inside the room.

"Okay, then, holler if you need me," she said as she walked back to her office.

Ahti and I piled the rickety trolley with as many supplies as we thought we would need and pushed through the double glass doors. The doors closed behind us. And then it happened.

Sure enough, it was Covid, sitting on the operating table, smoking a cigarette, and playing solitaire.

"I've been waiting for you," he growled, eyeing me. I felt my heart, that reliable, old ticker, jump up into my throat.

"I can't breathe," I whispered. Bending over, my face in front of my knees, I yanked off my face shield and masks.

I imagined Covid blowing smoke rings with little Covids wafting down to finish me off.

Ahti's feet came into view.

"Put your stuff back on," he said leaning over to look at me. "Put your stuff back on," he said again tapping my shoulder.

Kicking around in the recesses of my mind was the awareness that this Covid scenario could not be real.

My mouth fell open like a landed fish sucking for oxygen.

Ahti was getting impatient. "Get up," he said, "c'mon." He stood up. "C'mon," he said gently nudging my shoulder with his knee.

A quick breath reached my lungs. A few more breaths . . . I stood up. I put my stuff back on.

Despite his stubborn reluctance, Ahti's cleaning skills were top notch. He started in the far corner of the room and meticulously scrubbed everything he could get his hands on, including the negative air pressure caterpillar. I had to admit that for Ahti, who had never cleaned a Covid room, this OR was a doozy.

I couldn't help him with the room because I found I had a big cleaning job of my own. There were ten lead aprons lying on top of one of the stainless-steel tables. These are used to protect staff from radiation. I had to clean and sanitize each one of them.

Ahti came over to look at the aprons. He pulled his masks down to talk to me. "Don't do it." He looked them over. "Blood," he said pointing to numerous brown spots, "blood, blood, blood. The employees who wore these should clean them."

He was right. These aprons should have been cleaned by the employees who wore them. Before Covid, a housekeeper rarely had to clean up blood, feces, urine, and other body fluids because the nurses took care of that. But Covid changed everything, and now housekeepers were responsible for cleaning these spills if nursing didn't have the time to take care of them.

"Look, he said," pointing his finger at the far wall and the wall next to it. "Blood." Ahti trudged over there, rubbed off the blood, and sanitized the area.

The average lead apron weighs between ten and fifteen pounds. But a few of the ones in front of me may have been closer to twenty. Bigger people need bigger aprons.

Cleaning these contraptions was complicated because of the Velcro attachments at the neck, the waist, the sides, and along the back of each apron. The wipes we use to clean are similar to baby wipes, so dragging these wipes over Velcro was like cleaning a bed of nails with a tissue.

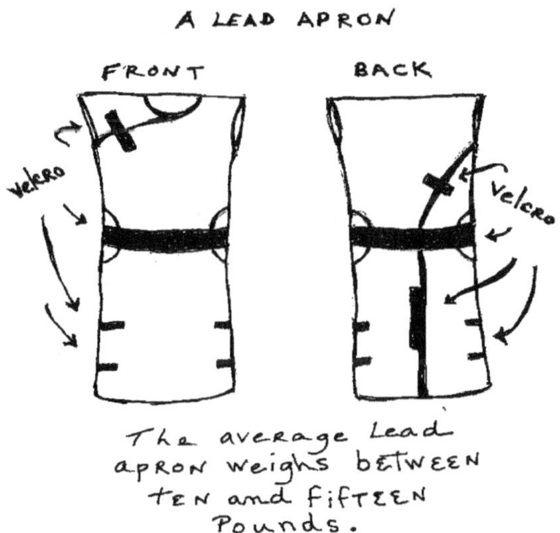

The average Lead apron weighs between ten and fifteen Pounds.

We had been in the room for more than sixty minutes when Prana stuck her head in the door, "Kids, we need this room in fifteen minutes."

Inside the OR, as per protocol, we removed our gloves and gowns and put them into a red hazard garbage bag. There were six more bags of garbage that we had filled while cleaning, and we pushed them out through the double doors, most of them red hazard bags.

We stepped out of the room, where I doubled all the bags while Ahti did the swan thing. After taking off the rest of our PPE and sanitizing it, Ahti took the garbage to the nearby garbage storage room. Everything in that room is collected by one of the housekeepers hourly and then it's brought to the back of the hospital for quick disposal.

There are three types of garbage every housekeeper brings to the garbage storage room after cleaning a room: hazardous red bags; general trash in clear bags; and dirty linen, also in clear bags. Early in the surge, the dirty linen was put into red hazard bags and thrown out. But Jermaine convinced the hospital that the EVS and the laundry were able to sanitize and recycle the linen.

I sanitized Prana's trolley, and we returned it to her. I thanked her profusely while Ahti ogled her as much as one can ogle while wearing a mask.

Hungry and ready for lunch, we walked the long mile to his locker to store the cart for later. And then Ahti did something I didn't expect. Holding up his bag of precious PPE over a wide-mouthed trash can, he looked directly at me and dropped it in.

"I cannot clean Covid," he said. "My daughter and grandson live with me. If my daughter finds out, she will be angry and take my grandson away."

Aha! Now I understood Ahti. Now I understood his resistance to cleaning Covid. One sniff of Covid on Ahti's breath after work and his daughter would head for the hills with that kid slung over her shoulder, waving goodbye to grandpa.

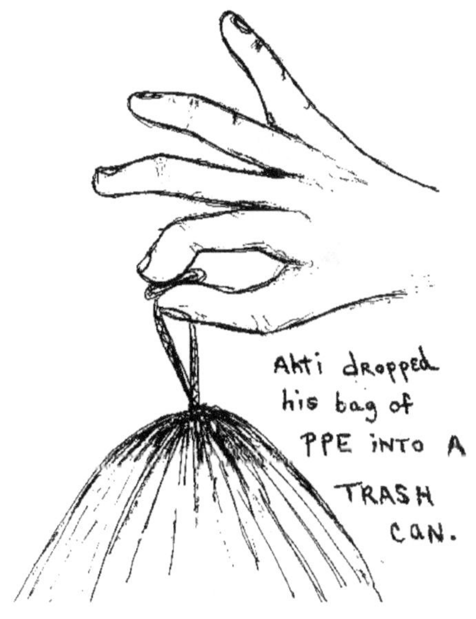

In Saints' Hospital the housekeepers, nurses, nursing assistants, physicians, unit clerks, and furloughs—basically any employee under its roof—were at risk for being shunned by family, friends, and neighbors due to our proximity to Covid.

Hospital workers were being praised as heroes during this pandemic. But in real life, lots of the people with whom I worked were shunned by family and friends. Being unwanted brought about great suffering.

Think about it.

Covid waits in the hospital lobby for every employee who walks through that door. Hissing hello, Covid wraps his fingers around their throats and hangs on to them throughout their shift.

Then imagine that employee, after his/her shift, going home and sitting alone.

One sniff of Covid and Ahti's daughter would head for the hills with that kid waving goodbye to him.

Here are just a few situations they endured:

- "I don't want him in my house. He works in a hospital."

- "Don't invite her to the BBQ. I know it's going to be in the backyard, but I still don't want her here."
- "Don't go for a walk with him."
- A divorced man in front of a judge, "I need to keep the kids with me because I can't risk having her near them. Please order that she has no visitation with the kids at all until this pandemic is over." The judge ruled in the man's favor.
- "He left homemade cookies outside our front door. Throw them in the garbage but put gloves on before you touch them."
- A physician to her partner: "I'll go live in a hotel."
- To toddlers: "Daddy will be in the basement, and we can leave dinner in front of the basement door for him."

Yup. Covid pushed lots of frontline heroes into dark, empty places. Adding insult to injury, even employees' pets were shunned because people believed that Covid might be hiding in their fur or feathers.

My husband was accepting of the fact that Covid and I were spending lots of long nights together. He also knew Covid was dying to meet him.

"What does your husband like to do?" Covid asked me one night, leaning on the housekeeping cart, cleaning his ear with a Q-tip.

"He likes to sit on our couch, watch TV, and eat popcorn," I told him.

"Me too!"

For a moment I imagined Covid barging into our apartment, telling my husband to move over to make room for him on the couch, grabbing the remote and the popcorn.

My Finnish husband would look at Covid for a long time, let out a sigh, and say, “Covid, this is the story of my life… pass the popcorn.”

EPILOGUE

THE FIRST DAY I RETURNED to my dietitian job, I stood in my office and looked around. Who slammed the brakes on the run-away train I had been riding but never bought a ticket for?

I received a letter from the hospital administration asking furloughs to get a Covid antibody blood test. I tested negative, which probably means that I was not exposed to Covid in the hospital even though I was swimming in it. I think that I was protected from getting Covid because of the PPE I wore while working, especially the masks. The strict after-work ritual that I designed probably helped protect me and my husband as well.

I was called a hero by some people in the office, but I knew I wasn't a hero – just a jumpy chicken in a housekeeper uniform. I knew who the real heroes were – and every one of them was still in Saints' Hospital pounding Covid into ash.

Unfortunately, during all the community celebrations for first responders, I saw only one sign of gratitude for the housekeepers. There should have been thousands of those signs.

I never really learned how to be a good housekeeper, but I did learn one thing: If it weren't for housekeepers, Covid would never go away. And I hope you, dear reader, have learned that too.